AF530059

YOUR WORD IS YOUR WAND

A Sequel to The Game of Life and How to Play It

FLORENCE SCOVEL SHINN

CLASSY
PUBLISHING

YOUR WORD IS YOUR WAND
by Florence Scovel Shinn
Published by Classy Publishing, 2025

www.classypublishing.com
info@classypublishing.com

ISBN: 978-93-5522-973-1

No part of this publication may be reproduced, stored in a retrieval system, or transmitted, in any form or by any means, electronic, mechanical, photocopying, recording or otherwise, without the prior permission of the publisher.

For more books
Please visit *classypublishing.com*

CONTENTS

YOUR WORD IS YOUR WAND

Man's word is his wand filled with magic and power!

Jesus Christ emphasized the power of the word; "By thy words thou shalt be justified and by thy words thou shalt be condemned," and "death and life are in power of the tongue."

So man has power to change an unhappy condition by waving over it the wand of his word.

In the place of sorrow appears joy, in the place of sickness appears health, in the place of lack appears plenty.

For example: A woman came for a treatment for prosperity. She possessed just two dollars in the world.

I said: "We bless the two dollars and know that you have the magic purse of the Spirit; it can never be depleted; as money goes out, immediately money comes in, under grace in perfect ways.

I see it always crammed, jammed with money: yellow bills, green bills, pink checks, blue checks, white checks, gold, silver and currency. I see it bulging with abundance!"

She replied: "I feel my bag heavy with money," and was so filled with faith that she gave me one of her dollars as a love offering. I did not dare refuse it and see lack for her, as it was important that I hold the picture of plenty.

Shortly afterwards she was made a gift of six thousand dollars. Fearless faith and the spoken word brought it to pass.

The affirmation of the magic purse is very powerful, as it brings a vivid picture to the mind. It is impossible not to see your purse or wallet filled with money when using the words, "crammed, jammed."

The imaging faculty is the creative faculty and it is important to choose words which bring a flash of the fulfillment of the demand.

Never force a picture by visualizing; let the Divine Idea flash into your conscious mind; then the student is working according to the Divine Design.

(See *The Game of Life and How to Play It*)

Jesus Christ said: "Ye shall know the Truth and the Truth shall make you free."

This means that man must know the Truth of every situation which confronts him.

There is no Truth in lack or limitation. *He waves over it the wand of His Word and the wilderness rejoices and blossoms as the rose.*

Fear, doubt, anxiety, anger, resentment pull down the cells of the body, shock the nervous system and are the causes of disease and disaster.

Happiness and health must be earned by absolute control of the emotional nature.

Power moves but is never moved. When man stands calm and serene, has a good appetite, feels contented and happy when appearances are against him, he has reached mastery. Then he has power to "rebuke the winds and the waves," to control conditions.

His word is his wand and he transmutes apparent failure into success.

He knows his universal supply is endless and immediate and all his needs manifest instantly on the external.

For example, a woman at sea awoke in the morning hearing the fog-horns blowing. A dense fog had settled on the ocean with no apparent signs of clearing. She immediately spoke the word: "There are no fogs in Divine Mind, so let the fog be lifted! I give thanks for the sun!"

Soon the sun came out, for man has dominion over "the elements—over all created things."

Every man has power to lift the fog in his life. It may be a fog of lack of money, love, happiness or health.

Give thanks for the sun!

SUCCESS

There are certain words or pictures which impress the subconscious mind.

For example: A man called asking me to speak the word for his right work.

I gave him the statement: "Behold I have set before thee the open door of destiny and no man shall shut it!"

It didn't seem to make much impression, so I was inspired to add: "And no man shall shut it for it is *nailed back!*"

The man was electrified and went out walking on air. Within a few weeks he was called to a distant city to fill a wonderful position which came about in a miraculous way.

I give another example of a woman who fearlessly followed a "hunch."

She was working for a small salary when she read my book, *The Game of Life and How to Play It*. The thought came in a flash, to start in business for herself and open a Tearoom and Candy Shop.

The idea staggered her at first, but it persisted, so she boldly went forth and procured a shop and assistants.

She "spoke the word for supply," for she did not have money to back her enterprise. It came in miraculous ways, and the shop opened!

From the first day it was filled with people, and now it is "crammed jammed"; they stand in line and wait.

One day, being a holiday, her assistants became gloomy and said they could not expect to do much business. My student, however, replied that God was her supply and every day was a good day.

In the afternoon an old friend came in to see the shop and bought a two pound box of candy. He gave her a check and when she looked at it she found it was for a hundred dollars. So it was indeed a good day! One hundred dollars for a box of candy!

She says every morning she enters the shop with wonder and gives thanks that she had the fearless faith that wins!

AFFIRMATIONS

The decks are now cleared for Divine Action and my own comes to me under grace in a magical way.

———

I now let go of worn-out conditions and worn-out things.

Divine order is established in my mind, body and affairs.

"Behold, I make all things new."

———

My seeming impossible good now comes to pass, the unexpected now happens!

———

The "four winds of success" now blow to me my own.

From North, South, East and West comes my endless good.

———

The Christ in me is risen, I now fulfill my destiny.

———

Endless good now comes to me in endless ways.

———

I clap my cymbals and rejoice, for Jehovah goes before me making clear, easy and successful my way!

———

I give thanks for my whirlwind success.

I sweep all before me for I work with the Spirit and follow the Divine Plan of my life.

———

My Spiritual Sporting blood is up! I am more than equal to this situation.

———

I am awake to my good, and gather in the harvest of endless opportunities.

———

I am harmonious, poised and magnetic.

I now draw to myself *my own*. My power is God's power and is irresistible!

———

Divine order is now established in my mind, body and affairs.

I see clearly and act quickly and my greatest expectations come to pass in a miraculous way.

———

There is no competition on the Spiritual plane. What is rightfully mine *is given me under grace*.

———

I have within me an undiscovered country, which is revealed to me now, in the name of Jesus Christ.

———

Behold! I have set before thee the open door of Destiny and no man shall shut it, for it is *nailed back.*

———

The tide of Destiny has turned and everything comes my way.

———

I banish the past and now live in the wonderful now, where happy surprises come to me each day.

———

There are no lost opportunities in Divine Mind, as one door shut *another door opened.*

———

I have a magical work in a magical way, I give magical service for magical pay.

———

The genius within me is now released. I now fulfill my destiny.

———

I make friends with hindrances and every obstacle becomes a stepping-stone. Every-thing in the Universe, visible and invisible, is working to bring to me my own.

———

I give thanks that the walls of Jericho fall down and all lack, limitation and failure are wiped out of my consciousness in the name of Jesus Christ.

———

I am now on the royal road of Success, Happiness and Abundance, all the traffic goes my way.

———

I will not weary of well-doing, for when I least expect it I shall reap.

———

Jehovah goes before me and the battle is won!

All enemy thoughts are wiped out.

I am victorious in the name of Jesus Christ.

———

There are no obstacles in Divine Mind, therefore, there is nothing to obstruct my good.

———

All obstacles now vanish from my pathway.

Doors fly open, gates are lifted and I enter the Kingdom of fulfillment, under grace.

———

Rhythm, harmony and balance are now established in my mind, body and affairs.

———

New fields of Divine activity now open for me and these fields are white with the harvest.

———

Man's will is powerless to interfere with God's will. God's will is now done in my mind, body and affairs.

———

God's plan for me is permanent and cannot be budged.

I am true to my *heavenly vision.*

———

"The Divine Plan of my life now takes shape in definite, concrete experiences leading to my heart's desire."

———

I now draw from the Universal Substance, with irresistible power and determination, that which is mine by Divine Right.

———

I do not resist this situation. I put it in the hands of Infinite Love and Wisdom. *Let the Divine idea now come to pass.*

———

My good now flows to me in a steady, unbroken, ever-increasing stream of success, happiness and abundance.

———

There are no lost opportunities in the Kingdom.

As one door shuts another door opens.

———

"There is nothing to fear for there is no power to hurt."

I walk up to the lion on my pathway and find an angel in armor, and victory in the name of Jesus Christ.

———

I am in perfect harmony with the working of the law. I stand aside and let Infinite Intelligence make easy and successful my way.

———

The ground I am on is holy ground; The ground I am on is successful ground.

———

New fields of Divine Activity now open for me.

Unexpected doors fly open, unexpected channels are free.

———

What God has done for others He can do for me and more!

———

I am as necessary to God as He is to me, for I *am* the channel to bring *His plan to pass.*

———

I do not limit God by seeing limitation in myself. With God and myself all things are possible.

———

Giving precedes receiving and my gifts to others precede God's gifts to me.

———

Every man is a golden link in the chain of my good.

———

My poise is built upon a rock. I see clearly and act quickly.

———

God cannot fail, so I cannot fail. "The warrior within me" has already won.

———

Thy Kingdom come in me, Thy will be done in me and my affairs.

PROSPERITY

(See also *The Game of Life and How to Play It.*)

Man comes into the world financed by God, with all that he desires or requires already on his pathway.

This supply is released through faith and the *Spoken Word.*

"If thou canst believe, all things are possible."

For example: A woman came to me one day, to tell me of her experience in using an affirmation she had read in my book, *The Game of Life and How to Play It.*

She was without experience but desired a good position on the stage. She took the affirmation: "Infinite Spirit, open the way for my great abundance. I am an irresistible magnet for all that belongs to me by Divine Right."

She was given a very important part in a successful opera.

She said: "It was a miracle, due to that affirmation, which I repeated hundreds of times."

AFFIRMATIONS

I now draw from the abundance of the spheres my immediate and endless supply.

All channels are free!

All doors are open!

———

I now release the gold-mine within me. I am linked with an endless golden stream of prosperity which comes to me under grace in perfect ways.

———

Goodness and mercy shall follow me all the days of my life and I shall dwell in the house of abundance forever.

———

My God is a God of plenty and I now receive all that I desire or require, and more.

———

All that is mine by Divine Right is now released and reaches me in great avalanches of abundance, under grace in miraculous ways.

———

My supply is endless, inexhaustible and immediate and comes to me under grace in perfect ways.

———

All channels are free and all doors fly open for my immediate and endless, Divinely Designed supply.

My ships come in over a calm sea, under grace in perfect ways.

———

I give thanks that the millions which are mine by Divine Right, now pour in and pile up under grace in perfect ways.

———

Unexpected doors fly open, unexpected channels are free, and endless avalanches of abundance are poured out upon me, under grace in perfect ways.

———

I spend money under direct inspiration wisely and fearlessly, knowing my supply is endless and immediate.

———

I am fearless in letting money go out, knowing God is my immediate and endless supply.

HAPPINESS

In that wonderful moving picture, "The Thief of Bagdad," we were told in letters of light that *happiness must be earned!*

It is earned through perfect control of the emotional nature.

There can be no happiness where there is fear, apprehension or dread. With *perfect faith in God* comes a feeling of *security* and *happiness.*

When man *knows* that there is an invincible power that protects him and all that he loves, and brings to him every righteous desire of the heart, he relaxes all nervous tension and is happy and satisfied.

He is undisturbed by adverse appearances, knowing that *Infinite Intelligence* is protecting his interests and utilizing every situation to bring his good to pass.

"I will make a way in the wilderness and rivers in a desert."

Uneasy lies the head that wears a frown. Anger, resentment, ill-will, jealousy and revenge rob man of his happiness and bring sickness, failure and poverty in their wake.

Resentment has ruined more homes than drink and killed more people than war.

For example: There was a woman who was healthy and happy and married to a man she loved.

The man died and left part of his estate to a relative. The woman was filled with resentment. She lost weight, was unable to do her work, developed gall-stones and became very ill.

A metaphysician called upon her one day. He said: "Woman, see what hate and resentment have done to you; they have caused hard stones to form in your body and only forgiveness and good-will can cure you."

The woman saw the Truth of the statement. She became harmonious and forgiving and regained her splendid health.

AFFIRMATIONS

I am now deluged with the happiness that was planned for me in the Beginning.

My barns are full, my cup flows over with joy.

———

My endless good now comes to me in endless ways.

———

I have a wonderful joy in a wonderful way, and my wonderful joy has come to stay.

———

Happy surprises come to me each day. "I look with wonder at that which is before me."

———

I walk boldly up to the lion on my pathway and find it is a friendly airedale.

———

I am harmonious, happy, radiant; detached from the tyranny of fear.

———

My happiness is built upon a rock. It is mine now and for all eternity.

———

My good now flows to me in a steady unbroken, ever-increasing stream of happiness.

———

My happiness is God's affair, therefore, no one can interfere.

———

As I am one with God I am now one with my heart's desire.

———

I give thanks for my permanent happiness, my permanent health, my permanent wealth, my permanent love.

———

I am harmonious, happy and Divinely magnetic, and now draw to me my ships over a calm sea.

———

God's ideas for me are perfect and permanent.

———

My heart's desire is a perfect idea in Divine Mind, incorruptible and indestructible, and now comes to pass, under grace in a magical way.

LOVE

With love usually comes terrific fear. Nearly every woman comes into the world with a mythical woman in the back of her mind who is to rob her of her love.

She has been called "the other woman." Of course it comes from woman's belief in duality. So long as she visualizes interference, it will come.

It is usually very difficult for a woman to see herself loved by the man she loves, so these affirmations are to impress the truth of the situation upon her subconscious mind, for in reality there is *only oneness.*

(See *The Game of Life and How to Play It.*)

AFFIRMATIONS

As I am one with God, the Undivided One, I am one with my undivided love and undivided happiness.

———

The Light of the Christ within now wipes out all fear, doubt, anger and resentment. God's love pours through me, an irresistible magnetic current. I see only perfection and draw to me my own.

———

Divine Love, through me, now dissolves all seeming obstacles and makes clear, easy and successful my way.

———

I love everyone and everyone loves me. My apparent enemy becomes my friend, a golden link in the chain of my good.

———

I am at peace with myself and with the whole world. I love everyone and everyone loves me.

The flood gates of my good now open.

MARRIAGE

Unless marriage is built upon the rock of *oneness* it cannot stand; "Two souls with but a single thought, two hearts that beat as one."

The poet understood this, for unless man and wife are living the same thoughts (or living in the same thought world), they must inevitably drift apart.

Thought is a tremendous vibratory force and man is drawn to his thought creations.

For example: A man and woman married and were apparently happy. The man became successful and his tastes improved, but the wife still lived in a limited consciousness.

Whenever the man bought anything he went to the best shops and selected what he needed regardless of price.

Whenever the wife went out she haunted the Five and Ten Cent Stores.

He was living (in thought), on Fifth Avenue and her thought world was on Third Avenue.

Eventually the break and separation came.

We see this so often in the cases of rich and successful men who desert their faithful, hardworking wives later in life.

The wife must keep pace with her husband's taste and ambitions and live in his thought world, for *where* a man thinketh in his heart *there is he.*

There is for each person his "other half' or divine selection.

These two are one in their thought worlds. These are the two "whom God has joined together and no man shall (or can) part asunder." "The twain shall be made one," for in the superconscious mind of each is the same Divine Plan.

AFFIRMATION

I give thanks that the marriage made in heaven is now made manifest upon earth.

"The twain shall be made one" now and for all eternity.

FORGIVENESS

AFFIRMATIONS

I forgive everyone and everyone forgives me. The gates swing open for my good.

———

I call on the law of forgiveness. I am free from mistakes and the consequences of mistakes. I am under grace and not under karmic law.

———

Though my mistakes be as scarlet, I shall be washed whiter than snow.

———

What didn't happen in the Kingdom never happened anywhere.

WORDS OF WISDOM

AFFIRMATIONS

"Faith without nerve is dead."

———

There is never a slip 'twixt the right cup and the right lip.

———

Never look or you'd never leap.

———

God works in unexpected places, through unexpected people, at unexpected times, His wonders to perform.

———

Power moves but is never moved.

———

Loving your neighbor means not to limit your neighbor in word, thought or deed.

———

"Never argue with a hunch."

———

Christopher Columbus followed a hunch.

———

The Kingdom of Heaven is the realm of perfect ideas.

———

It is dark before the dawn but the dawn never fails. Trust in the dawn.

———

When in doubt play trumps, *do the fearless thing.*

———

It is the fearless things that count.

———

Never do today what intuition says to do tomorrow.

———

It's a great life if you don't reason.

———

Regard your neighbor as yourself.

———

Never hinder another's hunch.

———

Selfishness binds and blocks. Every loving and unselfish thought has in it the germ of success.

———

Be not weary of make-believing. When you least expect it you shall reap.

———

Faith is elastic. Stretch it to the end of your demonstration.

———

Before you call you are answered, for the supply precedes the demand.

———

What you do for others you are doing for yourself.

———

Every act committed while angry or resentful brings unhappy reaction.

———

Sorrow and disappointment follow in the wake of deceit and subterfuge. The way of the transgressor is hard. "No good thing will be withheld from him who *walks uprightly*."

———

There is no power in evil. It is nothing; therefore can only come to nothing.

———

Fear and impatience demagnetize. Poise magnetizes.

———

Drown the reasoning mind with your affirmation. Jehoshaphat clapped his cymbals so that he wouldn't hear himself think.

———

All bondage is an illusion of the race consciousness. There is always a way out of every situation, under grace. Every man is free to do the will of God.

———

Sure-ism is stronger than Optimism.

———

"Divine ideas never conflict."

———

It is dangerous to stop in the middle of a *hunch.*

Infinite Spirit is never too late.

FAITH

Hope looks forward, *Faith knows it has already received and acts accordingly.*

In my classes I often emphasize the importance of digging ditches (or preparing for the thing asked for) which shows active faith and brings the demonstration to pass.

(See *The Game of Life and How to Play It.*)

A man in my class, whom I called "the life of the party," because he always tried to find a question I couldn't answer, but he never succeeded, asked: "Why is it then, a lot of women who prepare Hope Chests never get married?" I replied: "Because it is a Hope Chest and not a *Faith Chest*."

The prospective bride also violates law in telling others about it. Her friends come in and sit on the Hope Chest and either doubt or hope she'll never succeed.

"Pray to thy Father which is in secret, and thy Father which seeth in secret shall reward thee openly."

The student should never talk of a demonstration until it "has jelled," or comes to pass on the external.

So a Hope Chest should become a Faith Chest and be kept from the public eye, and the word spoken for the Divine Selection of a husband, under grace in a perfect way.

Those whom God hath joined together no thought can put asunder.

AFFIRMATIONS

Adverse appearances work for my good, for God utilizes every person and every situation to bring to me my heart's desire.

"Hindrances are friendly" and obstacles spring boards!

I now jump into my good!

———

As I am one with the *Undivided One*, I am one with my undivided good.

———

As the needle in the compass is true to the north, what is rightfully mine is true to me.

I am the North!

———

"I am now linked by an invisible, unbreakable magnetic cord with all that belongs to me by Divine Right!

———

Thy Kingdom is come, Thy will is done in me and my affairs.

———

Every plan my Father in heaven has not planned is dissolved and obliterated and the Divine Design of my life now comes to pass.

———

What God has given me can never be taken from me for His gifts are for all eternity.

———

My faith is built upon a rock and my heart's desire now comes to pass, under grace in a miraculous way.

———

I see my good in a golden glow of glory. I see my fields shining white with the harvest.

———

God is my unfailing and immediate supply of all good.

———

I am poised and powerful, my greatest expectations are realized in a miraculous way.

———

I water my wilderness with faith and suddenly it blossoms as the rose.

———

I now exercise my fearless faith in three ways—by thinking, speaking and acting.

I am unmoved by appearances, therefore appearances move.

———

I stand steadfast, immovable, giving thanks for my seeming impossible good to come to pass, for I know, with God, it is easy of accomplishment, and His time is *now*.

———

God's plans for me are built upon a rock. What was mine in the beginning, is mine now and ever shall be mine.

———

I *know* there is nothing to defeat God, therefore, there is nothing to defeat me.

———

I wait patiently on the Lord, I trust in Him, I fret not myself because of evil doers (for every man is a golden link in the chain of my good) and He now gives to me the desires of my heart! (See 37th Psalm.)

———

I have now the fearless faith of the Christ within. At my approach barriers vanish and obstacles disappear.

———

I am steadfast, immovable, for the fields are already white with the harvest. My fearless faith in God now brings the Divine Design of my life to pass.

———

All fear is now banished in the name of Jesus Christ, for I know there is no power to hurt.

God is the one and only power.

———

I am in perfect harmony with the working of the law, for I know that Infinite Intelligence knows nothing of obstacles, time or space. It knows only completion.

———

God works in unexpected and magic ways His wonders to perform.

———

I now prepare for the fulfillment of my heart's desire. I show God I believe His promise will be kept.

———

I now dig my ditches deep with faith and understanding and my heart's desire comes to pass in a surprising way.

———

My ditches will be filled at the right time, bringing all that I have asked for, and more!

———

I now "put to flight the army of the aliens" (negative thoughts). They feed on fear and starve on faith.

———

God's ideas cannot be moved, therefore, what is mine by Divine Right will always be with me.

———

I give thanks that I now receive the righteous desires of my heart.

Mountains are removed, valleys exalted and every crooked place made straight.

I am in the Kingdom of fulfillment.

———

I have perfect confidence in God and God has perfect confidence in me.

———

God's promises are built upon a rock. As I have asked I *must* receive.

———

"Let me never wander from my heart's desire."

———

I do not limit the Holy One of Israel, in word, thought or deed.

With God all things are easy and possible now.

———

I now stand aside and watch God work.

It interests me to see how quickly and easily He brings the desires of my heart to pass.

———

Before I called I was answered and I now gather in my harvest in a remarkable way.

———

He who watches over my heart's desire "Neither slumbers nor sleeps."

———

Seeming impossible doors now open, seeming impossible channels are free, in the name of *Jesus Christ.*

———

My good is a perfect and permanent idea in Divine Mind, and must manifest for there is nothing to prevent.

———

I cast every burden on the Christ within and I go free!

(See *The Game of Life and How to Play It.*)

LOSS

If man loses anything it shows there is a belief of loss in his subconscious mind. As he erases this false belief, the article, or its equivalent will appear on the external.

For example: A woman lost a silver pencil in a theatre. She made every effort to find it but it was not returned.

She denied loss, taking the affirmation: "I deny loss, there is no loss in Divine Mind, therefore I cannot lose that pencil. I will receive it or its equivalent."

Several weeks elapsed. One day she was with a friend who wore about her neck on a cord, a beautiful gold pencil, who turned to her and said: "Do you want this pencil? I paid fifty dollars for it at Tiffany's."

The woman was aghast, and replied (almost forgetting to thank her friend) "Oh! God aren't you wonderful! The silver pencil wasn't good enough for me!"

Man can only lose what doesn't belong to him by Divine Right, or isn't good enough for him.

AFFIRMATIONS

There is no loss in Divine Mind, therefore, I cannot lose anything that is rightfully mine.

Infinite Intelligence is never too late! Infinite Intelligence knows the way of recovery.

———

There is no loss in Divine Mind, therefore, I cannot lose anything which belongs to me.

It will be restored or I receive its equivalent.

DEBT

If a man is in debt or people owe him money, it shows that a belief of debt is in his subconscious mind.

This belief must be neutralized in order to change conditions.

For example: A woman came to me saying a man had owed her a thousand dollars for years which she could not compel him to pay.

I said: "You must work on yourself, not the man," and gave her this statement: "I deny debt, there is no debt in Divine Mind, no man owes me anything, all is squared. I send that man love and forgiveness."

In a few weeks she received a letter from him saying he intended sending the money and in about a month came the thousand dollars.

If the student owes money, change the statement: "There is no debt in Divine Mind, therefore, I owe no man anything, all is *squared.*

All my obligations are now wiped out, under grace in a perfect way."

AFFIRMATIONS

I deny debt, there is no debt in Divine Mind, therefore, I owe no man anything.

All obligations are now wiped out under grace in a miraculous way.

———

I deny debt, there is no debt in Divine Mind, no man owes me anything, all is squared. I send forth love and forgiveness.

SALES

A woman who lived in a country town wished to sell her house and furniture. It was in the winter with snow so deep it was almost impossible for cars or wagons to reach her door.

As she had asked God to sell her furniture to the right person for the right price she was unmindful of appearances.

She polished the furniture, pushed it into the middle of the room and prepared to sell it.

She said: "I never looked out of the window at the blizzard, I simply trusted God's promises."

In miraculous ways people drove up and all the furniture was sold, and the house also, without paying any commission to an agent.

Faith never looks out of the window at the blizzard, it simply prepares for the blessing asked for.

AFFIRMATION

I give thanks that this article (or property) is now sold to the right person or persons for the right price, giving perfect satisfaction.

INTERVIEWS

AFFIRMATIONS

There is no competition on the Spiritual plane. What is mine is given me, under grace.

———

I am identified in love with the Spirit of this person (or persons). God protects my interests and the Divine Idea now comes out of this situation.

GUIDANCE

Always on man's pathway is his message or his lead.

For example: A woman was much troubled over an unhappy situation. She thought to herself, "Will it ever clear up?"

Her maid was standing near and commenced to tell her of her experiences. The woman was too worried to be interested but listened patiently. The maid was saying: "I worked in a hotel once where there was a very amusing gardener, he always said such funny things. It had been raining for three days and I said to him: 'Do you think it will ever clear up?' And he replied, 'My God, doesn't it always clear up?'"

The woman was amazed! It was the answer to her thoughts. She said reverently, "Yes, with my God it always clears up!" Soon after, her problem did clear up in an unexpected way.

AFFIRMATIONS

Infinite Spirit, give me wisdom to make the most of my opportunities.

Never let me miss a trick.

———

I am always under direct inspiration. I know just what to do and give instant obedience to my intuitive leads.

———

My angel of destiny goes before me, keeping me in the Way.

———

All power is given unto me to be meek and lowly of heart.

I am willing to come last, therefore, I come first!

———

I now place my personal will upon the altar.

Your will, not my will; Your way not my way; Your time not my time—*and in the twinkling of an eye it is done!*

———

There are no mysteries in the Kingdom. Whatever I should know will now be revealed to me, under grace.

———

I am a perfect non-resistant instrument for God to work through, and His perfect plan for me now comes to pass in a magic way.

PROTECTION

AFFIRMATIONS

I am surrounded by the White Light of the Christ, through which nothing negative can penetrate.

———

I walk in the Light of the Christ and my fear giants dwindle into nothingness.

There is nothing to oppose my good.

MEMORY

AFFIRMATION

There is no loss of memory in Divine Mind, therefore, I recollect everything I should remember and I forget all that is not for my good.

THE DIVINE DESIGN

(*See also The Game of Life and How to Play It.*)

There is a Divine Design for each man!

Just as the perfect picture of the oak is in the acorn, the divine pattern of his life is in the super-conscious mind of man.

In the Divine Design there is no limitation, only health, wealth, love and perfect self-expression.

So on man's pathway there is always a Divine Selection. Each day he must live according to the Divine Plan or have unhappy reactions.

For example: A woman moved into a new apartment which she had almost furnished, when the thought came to her: "On that side of the room should stand a Chinese cabinet!

Not long after, she was walking by an antique shop. She glanced in and there stood a magnificent Chinese cabinet about eight feet high, elaborately carved.

She entered and asked the price. The salesman said it was worth a thousand dollars but the woman who owned it was willing to take less. The man added: "What will you offer for it?" The woman paused and the price "Two hundred dollars" came into her mind, so she answered: "Two hundred dollars." The man said he would let her know if the offer were satisfactory.

She did not want to cheat anyone or get anything which was not rightfully hers, so going home she said repeatedly: "*If it's mine I can't lose it and of it isn't mine, I don't want it.*" It was a snowy day and she said she emphasized her words by kicking the snow from right to left, clearing a pathway to her apartment.

Several days elapsed when she was notified that the woman was willing to sell the cabinet for two hundred dollars.

There is a supply for every demand, from Chinese cabinets to millions of dollars.

"Before ye call I shall answer," but, unless it is the Divinely Selected cabinet or millions they would never bring happiness.

"Except the Lord build the house, they labor in vain that build it." (Psalm 127-1.)

AFFIRMATIONS

I let go of everything not divinely designed for me, and the perfect plan of my life now comes to pass.

———

What is mine by Divine Right can never be taken from me.

God's perfect plan for me is built upon a rock.

———

I follow the magic path of intuition and find myself in my Promised Land, under grace.

———

My mind, body and affairs are now molded according to the Divine pattern within.

———

"God is the only power and that power is within me. There is only one plan, God's plan, and that plan now comes to pass."

———

"I give thanks that I now bring forth from the Universal Substance everything that satisfies all the righteous desires of my heart."

———

The divine Design of my life now comes to pass. I now fill the place that I can fill and no one else can fill. I now do the things which I can do and no one else can do.

———

I am fully equipped for the Divine Plan of my life; I am more than equal to the situation.

———

All doors now open for happy surprises and the Divine Plan of my life is speeded up under grace.

HEALTH

When man is harmonious and happy he is healthy! All sickness comes from sin or violation of Spiritual Law.

Jesus Christ said: "Be thou healed, your sins are forgiven."

Resentment, ill-will, hate, fear, etc., etc., tear down the cells of the body and poison the blood. (See *The Game of Life and How to Play It.*)

Accidents, old age and death itself, come from holding wrong mental pictures.

When man sees himself as God sees him, he will become a radiant being, timeless, birthless and deathless, for "God made man in His likeness and in His image."

AFFIRMATIONS

I deny fatigue, for there is nothing to tire me. I live in the Kingdom of eternal joy and absorbing interests.

My body is "the body electric," timeless and tireless, birthless and deathless.

Time and space are obliterated!

———

I live in the wonderful now, birthless and deathless!

I am one with *The One!*

———

Thou in me art:

> Eternal joy.
> Eternal youth.
> Eternal wealth.
> Eternal health.
> Eternal love.
> Eternal life.

———

I am a Spiritual Being—my body is perfect, made in His likeness and image.

The Light of the Christ now streams through every cell. I give thanks for my radiant health.

EYES

(Imperfect vision. Correspondences—Fear, suspicion, seeing obstacles. Watching for unhappy events to come to pass—living in the past or future—not living in the NOW.)

AFFIRMATIONS

The Light of the Christ now floods my eyeballs. I have the crystal clear vision of the Spirit. I see clearly and distinctly there are no obstacles on my pathway. I see clearly the fulfillment of my heart's desire.

———

I have the X-ray eye of the Spirit. I see through apparent obstacles. I see clearly the miracle come to pass.

———

I have the crystal clear vision of the Spirit, I see clearly the open road. There are no obstacles on my pathway. I now see miracles and wonders come to pass.

———

I give thanks for my perfect sight. I see God in every face, I see good in every situation.

———

I have the crystal clear vision of the Spirit. I look up and down and all around, for my good comes from North, South, East and West.

———

My eyes are God's eyes, perfect and flawless. The Light of the Christ floods my eyeballs and streams on my pathway. I see clearly there are no lions on my way, only angels and endless blessings.

ANAEMIA

(*Correspondence—Unfed desires—lack of happiness.*)

AFFIRMATION

I am nourished by the Spirit within. Every cell in my body is filled with light. I give thanks for radiant health and endless happiness. (*This statement may be used in the healing of any disease.*)

EARS

(Deafness—Correspondence—Strong personal will, stubbornness and a desire not to hear certain things.)

AFFIRMATION

My ears are the ears of Spirit. The Light of the Christ now streams through my ears dissolving all hardness or malformation.

I hear clearly the voice of intuition and give instant obedience.

I hear clearly glad tidings of great joy.

RHEUMATISM

(*Correspondence—Fault finding, criticism, etc.*)

AFFIRMATION

The Light of the Christ now floods my consciousness dissolving all acid thoughts.

I love everyone and everyone loves me.

I give thanks for my radiant health and happiness.

FALSE GROWTHS

(*Correspondence—Jealousy, hatred, resentment, fear, etc., etc.*)

AFFIRMATION

Every plant my Father in Heaven has not planted shall be rooted up. All false ideas in my consciousness are now obliterated. The Light of the Christ streams through every cell and I give thanks for my radiant health and happiness now and forevermore.

HEART DISEASE

(*Correspondence—Fear, Anger, etc.*)

AFFIRMATION

My heart is a perfect idea in Divine Mind and is now in its right place, doing its right work.

It is a happy heart, a fearless heart and a loving heart.

The Light of the Christ streams through every cell and I give thanks for my radiant health.

ANIMALS

(*Dog: for example*)

AFFIRMATIONS

I deny any appearance of disorder. This dog is a perfect idea in Divine Mind and now expresses God's perfect Idea of a perfect dog.

———

Infinite Intelligence illumines and directs this animal. It is a perfect idea in Divine Mind and is always in its right place.

THE ELEMENTS

Man is made in God's likeness and image (Imagination) and is given power and dominion over all created things.

He has power to "rebuke the winds and the waves," check floods or bring rain when it is needed.

There is a tribe of American Indians who live in the desert country and depend on the power of prayer only, to bring rain to water their crops.

They have a rain dance, which is a form of prayer, but no chief is allowed to take part who has any fear.

They give exhibitions of courage before they are admitted to the ceremonies.

A woman, who was an eye-witness, told me that out of a blue sky came *a deluge of rain; the sun still shining.*

FIRE

AFFIRMATION

Fire is man's friend and is always in its right place doing its right work.

DROUGHT

AFFIRMATION

There is no drought in Divine Mind. I give thanks for the right amount of rain to nourish these crops or garden.

I see clearly this gentle downpour and the manifestation is *now*.

STORMS

AFFIRMATION

The Christ within now rebukes the winds and the waves and there comes a great calm.

I see clearly peace established on land and sea.

JOURNEY

AFFIRMATION

I give thanks for the Divinely planned journey under Divinely planned conditions with the Divinely planned supply.

MISCELLANEOUS

The thing you dislike or hate will surely come upon you, for when man hates, he makes a vivid picture in the subconscious mind and it objectifies.

The only way to erase these pictures is through non-resistance.

(See *The Game of Life and How to Play It.*)

For example: A woman was interested in a man who told her repeatedly of his charming women cousins.

She was jealous and resentful and he passed out of her life.

Later on she met another man to whom she was much attracted. In the course of their conversation he mentioned some women cousins he was very fond of.

She resented it, then laughed, for here were her old friends "the cousins" back again.

This time she tried non-resistance. She blessed all the cousins in the Universe and sent them good-will, for she knew if she didn't, every man she met would be stocked up with women relations.

It was successful for she never heard cousins mentioned again.

This is the reason so many people have unhappy experiences repeated in their lives.

I knew a woman who bragged of her troubles. She would go about saying to people; "I know what trouble is!" and then wait for their words of sympathy.

Of course, the more she mentioned her troubles, the more she had, for by her words she "was condemned."

She should have used her words to neutralize her troubles instead of to multiply them.

For example—had she said repeatedly: "I cast every burden upon the Christ within and I go free," and not voiced her sorrows, they would have faded from her life, for "*by your words you are justified*."

———

"I will give to thee the land that thou *seest*."

Man is ever reaping on the external what he has sown in his thought world.

For example: A woman needed money and was walking along the street making the affirmation that God was her immediate supply.

She looked down and at her feet was a two dollar bill, which she picked up.

A man standing near (a watchman in a building), said to her: "Lady, did you pick up some money? I thought it was a piece of chewing-gum paper. A lot of people walked over it, but *when you came it opened up like a leaf.*"

The others, thinking lack, had passed over it, but at her words of faith it unfurled.

So with the opportunities in life—one man sees, another passes by.

———

"Faith without works (or action) is dead."

The student, in order to bring into manifestation the answer to his prayer must show *active faith.*

For example: A woman came to me asking me to speak the word for the renting of a room.

I gave her the statement: "I give thanks that the room is now rented to the right and perfect man for the right price, giving perfect satisfaction."

Several weeks elapsed but the room had not been rented.

I asked: "Have you shown active faith? Have you followed every hunch in regard to the room?" She replied: "I had a hunch to get a lamp for the room, but I decided I couldn't afford it." I said: "You'll never rent the room until you get the lamp, for in buying the lamp you are *acting your faith*, impressing the subconscious mind with *certainty*."

I asked: "What is the price of the lamp?" She answered: "Four dollars." I exclaimed: "Four dollars standing between you and the perfect man!"

She became so enthusiastic, she bought *two* lamps.

About a week elapsed and in walked the perfect man. He did not smoke and paid the rent in advance and fulfilled her ideal in every way.

Unless you become as a little child and dig your ditches you shall in no wise enter the Kingdom of manifestation.

(See *The Game of Life and How to Play It*.)

———

"Without the vision my people perish." Unless man has some objective, some Promised Land to look forward to, he begins to perish.

We see it so often in small country towns, in the men who sit around a stove all winter, who "Ain't got no ambition."

Within each one is an undiscovered country, a gold mine.

I knew a man in a country town called "Magnolia Charlie," because he always found the first magnolia in the spring.

He was a shoemaker, but every afternoon left his work to go to the station to meet the four-fifteen train, from a distant city.

They were the only romances in his life, the first magnolia and the four-fifteen train.

He felt vaguely the call of the vision in the superconscious mind.

No doubt, the Divine Design for him included travel and perhaps he was to become a genius in the plant world.

Through the spoken word the Divine Design may be released and each one fulfill his destiny.

"I now see clearly the perfect plan of my life. Divine enthusiasm fires me and I now fulfill my destiny."

The Spiritual attitude towards money is to know that God *is man's supply*, and that he draws it from the abundance of the spheres, through his faith and spoken word.

When man realizes this he loses all greed for money, and is fearless in letting it go out.

With his magic purse of the Spirit, his supply is *endless* and *immediate*, and he knows also that *giving* precedes *receiving*.

For example: "A woman came to me asking me to speak the word for five hundred dollars by the first of August. (It was then about the first of July.)

I knew her very well, and said: "The trouble with you is you don't *give* enough. You must open your channels of supply by *giving*."

She had accepted an invitation to visit a friend and did not want to go on account of the formality.

She said: "Please treat me to be polite for three weeks, and I want to get away as soon as possible, and be sure to speak the word for the five hundred dollars."

She went to the friend's house, was unhappy and restless and tried continually to leave, but was always persuaded to stay longer.

She remembered my advice, however, and gave the people about her presents. Whenever possible she made a little gift.

It was nearing the first of August and no signs of the five hundred dollars, and no way of escape from the visit.

The last day of July she said: "Oh God! maybe I haven't given enough!" So she tipped all the servants more than she had intended.

The first of August, her hostess said to her: "My dear, I want to make you a gift," and she handed her a check for five hundred dollars!

God works in unexpected ways his wonders to perform.

AFFIRMATIONS

God is incapable of separation or division; therefore, my good is incapable of separation or division. I am *one* with my undivided good.

———

All that is mine by Divine Right is now released and reaches me in a perfect way under Grace.

———

God's work is finished now and must manifest.

———

I serve only faith and my unlimited abundance is made manifest.

———

I am undisturbed by appearances. I trust in God—and He now brings to me the desires of my heart.

———

My good now overtakes me in a surprising way.

———

The Divine Plan of my life cannot be tampered with. It is incorruptible and indestructible. It awaits only my recognition.

———

There is no there—there is only here.

———

Reveal to me the way, let me see clearly the blessing which Thou hast given me.

———

Let Thy blessed will be done in me this day.

———

Hunches are my hounds of Heaven—they lead me in the perfect way.

———

All things I seek are now seeking me.

———

Divine Activity is now operating in my mind, body and affairs, whether I see it or not.

———

Since I am one with the Only Presence, I am one with my heart's desire.

———

I now have the single eye of the Spirit and see only completion.

———

I am a perfect idea in Divine Mind and I am always in my right place doing my right work at the right time for the right pay.

———

The Columbus in you will see you through.

———

I am an irresistible magnet for checks, bills and currency—for everything that belongs to me by Divine Right.

———

Thou in me art completion. As I have asked I must receive.

———

The law of God is the law of increase and I give thanks for increase under grace in perfect ways.

———

I dwell in a sea of abundance. I see clearly my inexhaustible supply. I see clearly just what to do.

———

My "World of the Wondrous" now swings into manifestation and I enter my Promised Land under grace!

Great peace have I who love thy law of nonresistance and nothing shall offend me.

———

Thou in me art Inspiration, Revelation and Illumination.

CONCLUSION

Nothing is too good
to be true

Nothing is too wonderful
to happen

Nothing is too good
to last

Choose the affirmation which appeals to you the most and *wave it over the situation which confronts you.*

It is your *magic wand*, for your *word* is God in *action.*

"It shall not return unto me void but shall accomplish that whereunto it is sent." (Isaiah 55-11.)

"But I say, have they not heard? Yes, verily, their sound went into all the earth and *their words unto the end of the world.*" (Romans 10-18.)

For more books
Please visit *classypublishing.com*